What's in this book

This book belongs to

T0351541

_____

奇妙的一星期 A wonderful week

学习内容 Contents

沟通 Communication

说出一星期的日子
Say the days of the week

说出活动名称
Say the names of some activities

生词 New words

★ 星期一	Monday	
★ 星期二	Tuesday	
★ 星期三	Wednesday	
★ 星期四	Thursday	
★ 星期五	Friday	
★ 星期六	Saturday	
★ 星期日	Sunday	

★ 看	to look, to see
★ 看书	to read a book
★ 朋友	friend
画画	to draw
踢足球	to play football
唱歌	to sing

背景介绍：
玲玲和爱莎是好朋友，
她们总是形影不离。

句式 Sentence patterns

星期三，她看书。
She reads books on Wednesday.

星期四，我们踢足球。
We play football on Thursday.

跨学科学习 Project

计划一周的活动并向朋友说一说
Plan and draw activities for one week and tell a friend about them

文化 Cultures

表达友情的不同方式
Different ways to show friendship

参考答案：
1 Yes, they look like very good friends in the photo.
2 Yes, Tony and Linda are my good friends./Yes, my pet Fluffy is my good friend.
3 Yes, we play basketball together on Saturdays./ No, we play together on Wednesdays only.

Get ready

1 Do you think Ling Ling and Elsa are good friends?

2 Do you have good friends?

3 Do you spend time with your friends on Saturdays?

故事大意：
在一个星期初，玲玲和爱莎的友情出现了小裂痕，
但两人很快就和好了，又开心地玩在了一起。

xīng qī yī
星期一

星期一，我们一起上学。

参考问题和答案：

1 It is the first school day of the week. What day is it today? (It is Monday.)

2 What are Ling Ling and Elsa doing? (They are going to school together.)

3 How do they look? (They look happy.)

星期二，我们不是朋友。

参考问题和答案：

1 It is the second school day of the week. What day is it today? (It is Tuesday.)

2 How do Ling Ling and Elsa look? (They look annoyed.)

3 What do you think happened between them? (They had an argument.)

xīng qī sān

星期三

星期三，她看书，我画画。

参考问题和答案：

1 It is the third school day of the week. What day is it today? (It is Wednesday.)

2 What are Ling Ling and Elsa doing? (Ling Ling is drawing and Elsa is taking a book from the bookshelf.)

3 Do Ling Ling and Elsa still care about each other? (Yes, they do.)

星期四，我们踢足球。

参考问题和答案：

1 It is the fourth school day of the week. What day is it today? (It is Thursday.)
2 What are Ling Ling and Elsa doing? (They are playing football.)
3 Ling Ling's team scored. How did they do that? (Ling Ling passed the ball to Elsa and Elsa kicked it into the goal.)

xīng qī wǔ
星期五

星期五，我们一起唱歌。

参考问题和答案：

1 It is the fifth school day of the week. What day is it today? (It is Friday.)
2 What are Ling Ling and Elsa doing? (They are singing.)

 3 How do they look? (They look happy.)

延伸活动：
问问学生有没有跟好朋友吵架的经历，
最后又是如何解决的。

xīng qī liù
星期六

提醒学生一星期有七天，星
期一到星期六，另外一天是
星期日，不是星期七。

xīng qī rì
星期日

星期六、星期日，我们是好朋友。

参考问题和答案：

1 What are Ling Ling and Elsa doing? (They are playing in the park.)

2 Do you think they are still angry at each other? (No, they are not. They are good friends again.)

Let's think

1 Number the pictures. Act out the story.

4

1

6

3

2

5

2 Suggest ways for Ling Ling and Elsa to be friends again on Tuesday. Draw your ideas in the bubbles.

参考答案：
1 两人面对面跟对方道歉。
2 给对方写小卡片，承认自己的错误，或谅解对方的错误。

New words

 1 Learn the new words.

星期一
唱歌

星期二
踢足球

星期三
看书

星期四
看书

星期五
画画

星期六
唱歌

星期日

朋友……

延伸活动：
学生说说图片中的人物一周的活动。如：星期一，玲玲唱歌。
星期二，伊森和艾文踢足球。……

2 Write the correct characters to complete the days of the week.

| 星期一 | 星期二 | 星期三 | 星期四 | 星期五 | 星期六 | 星期日 |

听听说说 Listen and say

03 **1** Listen and complete the exercises. 完成后，问问学生连出来的是什么图形。

1 Connect the days.

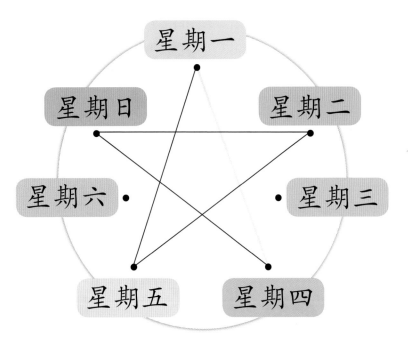

2 Write the correct day.

星期 ___六___

04 **2** Look at the pictures. Listen to

我们一起上学。

星期六，伊森画画，浩浩玩飞机。

第二题参考问题和答案：

1 What do Ethan and Ivan do on Mondays? (Ethan reads books. Ivan plays football.)

2 What do you and your friends do at the weekend? (We go to the park together./We make cakes together.)

...story and say.

3 Tick and say the correct sentences.

[✓] 星期五，浩浩踢足球。

[ ] 星期五，足球踢浩浩。

[ ] 我们唱歌星期日。

[✓] 星期日，我们唱歌。

Task

Draw your favourite activity for each day of the week. Tell your friend.

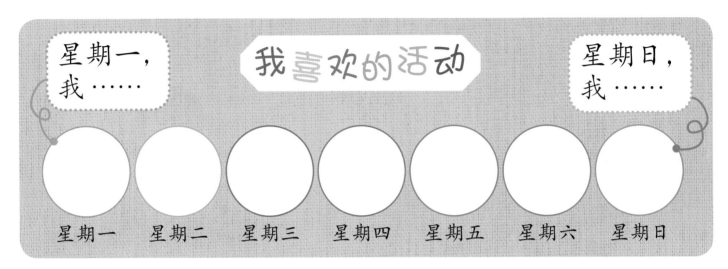

星期一，
我……

我喜欢的活动

星期日，
我……

星期一   星期二   星期三   星期四   星期五   星期六   星期日

Game

让学生观察一月至三月的日历，引导他们发现日历下方的星期对应的是日历上红圈中的日期。学生随后根据规律填空。

Check the calandar. Fill in the blanks with the correct characters.

JANUARY
S M T W T F S
            1 2 3
4 5 6 7 8 9 10
11 12 13 14 15 16 17
18 19 20 21 22 23 24
25 26 27 28 29 30 (31)

星期六

FEBRUARY
S M T W T F S
1 2 3 4 5 6 7
8 9 10 11 12 13 14
15 16 17 18 19 20 21
22 23 24 25 26 27 (28)

星期六

MARCH
S M T W T F S
1 2 3 4 5 6 7
8 9 10 11 12 13 14
15 16 17 18 19 20 21
22 23 24 25 26 27 28
29 30 (31)

星期二

APRIL
S M T W T F S
         1 2 3 4
5 6 7 8 9 10 11
12 13 14 15 16 17 18
19 20 21 22 23 24 25
26 27 28 29 30

星期 四

MAY
S M T W T F S
            1 2
3 4 5 6 7 8 9
10 11 12 13 14 15 16
17 18 19 20 21 22 23
24 25 26 27 28 29 30
31

星期 日

JUNE
S M T W T F S
   1 2 3 4 5 6
7 8 9 10 11 12 13
14 15 16 17 18 19 20
21 22 23 24 25 26 27
28 29 30

星期 二

JULY
S M T W T F S
         1 2 3 4
5 6 7 8 9 10 11
12 13 14 15 16 17 18
19 20 21 22 23 24 25
26 27 28 29 30 31

星期 五

AUGUST
S M T W T F S
                  1
2 3 4 5 6 7 8
9 10 11 12 13 14 15
16 17 18 19 20 21 22
23 24 25 26 27 28 29
30 31

星期 一

SEPTEMBER
S M T W T F S
      1 2 3 4 5
6 7 8 9 10 11 12
13 14 15 16 17 18 19
20 21 22 23 24 25 26
27 28 29 30

星期 三

OCTOBER
S M T W T F S
            1 2 3
4 5 6 7 8 9 10
11 12 13 14 15 16 17
18 19 20 21 22 23 24
25 26 27 28 29 30 31

星期 六

NOVEMBER
S M T W T F S
1 2 3 4 5 6 7
8 9 10 11 12 13 14
15 16 17 18 19 20 21
22 23 24 25 26 27 28
29 30

星期 一

DECEMBER
S M T W T F S
      1 2 3 4 5
6 7 8 9 10 11 12
13 14 15 16 17 18 19
20 21 22 23 24 25 26
27 28 29 30 31

星期 四

Song

Listen and sing.

一星期，有几天？

一星期，有七天。

一二三，四五六，

星期一到星期六，

没有星期七，

只有星期日。

过了星期日，

再到星期一。

延伸活动：

唱完歌后，全班玩一个接龙游戏，依次从"星期一"数到"星期日"，数完再从"星期一"开始。或可将难度提高，全班看着某一个月份的日历，根据老师指出的一天，一起说出该天是星期几。

星期一 星期二 星期三 星期四 星期五 星期六 星期日

课堂用语 Classroom language

继续。
Continue.

开始。
Start.

轮到你了。
It's your turn.

1 Revise and trace the stroke. 前面已经学过"横折"的笔画,这里再让学生温习一遍。

横折
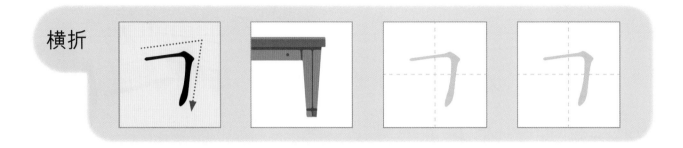

2 Colour 目 in the characters.

盼 相 盯 盾 省

3 How are these characters related to 目? Discuss with your friend.
告诉学生"眉"的英文释义,再让学生两人一组讨论。

眼睛

"目"就是"眼睛"的意思,而
"眉"长在眼睛的上方。

4 Trace and write the character.

---

5 Write and say.

浩浩指着燕子想让爸爸留意，问问学生应该用哪个字。

爸爸，你 看 ！

汉字小常识 Did you know?

Some characters are made up of left, middle and right components.

Colour the left component red, the middle component blue and the right component green.

红蓝绿
色色色

红蓝绿
色色色

红蓝绿
色色色

该结构中不同的字的左中右三个部件所占比例不一定相同。

多元学习 Connections

Cultures

1 Learn and talk about the different ways to show friendship with your friend.

In ancient China, the character for friend 友 was formed by two hands holding each other. Today, people still hold hands to show friendship.

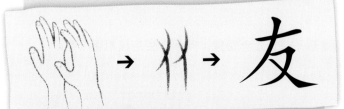

Besides holding hands, there are other ways to show friendship.

2 Colour the bookmarks for your friends.

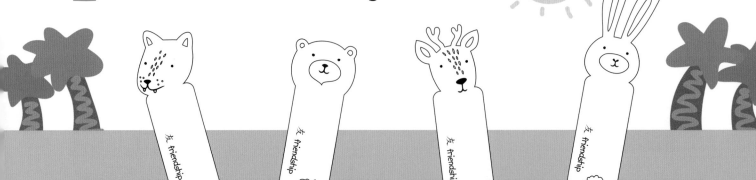

延伸活动：
完成涂色后，让每个学生分别用行动向四个同学表达友情，然后说说大家的感受。

1 Plan and draw your activities for a week.

2 Show your diary to your friends. Talk about your plan.

星期一，我……

星期二，我……

星期三，我……

星期四，我……

星期五，我……

星期六，我……

星期日，我……

参考答案：
星期一，我看书。星期二，我画画。星期三，我踢足球。星期四，我看书。
星期五，我和姐姐唱歌。星期六，我和三个男孩一起踢足球。星期日，我、
姐姐和小狗一起玩。

温习 Checkpoint

1 Follow the instructions on the cards. Arrange the days from Monday to Sunday and write the letters.

学生先将所有卡片按"星期一"至"星期日"的顺序排序，再完成卡片上的任务。

b, a, f, e, g, c, d

b 星期一

Read aloud.
星期一

a 星期二

踢足球
What is the activity?
Say in Chinese.

e 星期四

Read aloud.
我们是好朋友。

c 星期六

Trace the character.

d 星期日

唱歌
What are they doing?
Say in Chinese.

f 星期三

Say 'read books' in Chinese. 看书

g 星期五

Write the component.

评核方法：
学生两人一组，互相考察评价表内单词和句子的听说读写。交际沟通部分由老师朗读要求，学生再互相对话。如果达到了某项技能要求，则用色笔将星星或小辣椒涂色。

2 Work with your friend. Colour the stars and the chillies.

Words	说	读	写
星期一	☆	☆	🌶
星期二	☆	☆	🌶
星期三	☆	☆	🌶
星期四	☆	☆	🌶
星期五	☆	☆	🌶
星期六	☆	☆	🌶
星期日	☆	☆	🌶
看	☆	☆	☆
看书	☆	☆	🌶
朋友	☆	☆	🌶

Words and sentences	说	读	写
画画	☆	🌶	🌶
踢足球	☆	🌶	🌶
唱歌	☆	🌶	🌶
星期三，她看书。	☆	☆	🌶
星期四，我们踢足球。	☆	🌶	🌶

Say the days of the week	☆
Say the names of some activities	☆

3 What does your teacher say?

评核建议：
根据学生课堂表现，分别给予"太棒了！(Excellent!)"、
"不错！(Good!)"或"继续努力！(Work harder!)"的评价，
再让学生圈出左侧对应的表情，以记录自己的学习情况。

My teacher says ...

分享 Sharing

延伸活动：
1 学生用手遮盖英文，读中文单词，并思考单词意思；
2 学生用手遮盖中文单词，看着英文说出对应的中文单词；
3 学生两人一组，尽量运用中文单词复述故事。

Words I remember

星期一	xīng qī yī	Monday
星期二	xīng qī èr	Tuesday
星期三	xīng qī sān	Wednesday
星期四	xīng qī sì	Thursday
星期五	xīng qī wǔ	Friday
星期六	xīng qī liù	Saturday
星期日	xīng qī rì	Sunday

看	kàn	to look, to see
看书	kàn shū	to read a book
朋友	péng you	friend
画画	huà huà	to draw
踢足球	tī zú qiú	to play football
唱歌	chàng gē	to sing

Other words

上学	shàng xué	to go to school
好	hǎo	good

OXFORD
UNIVERSITY PRESS

Oxford University Press is a department of the University of Oxford.
It furthers the University's objective of excellence in research, scholarship,
and education by publishing worldwide. Oxford is a registered trade mark of
Oxford University Press in the UK and in certain other countries

Published in Hong Kong by
Oxford University Press (China) Limited
39th Floor, One Kowloon, 1 Wang Yuen Street, Kowloon Bay,
Hong Kong

Illustrated by Anne Lee and Wildman

Photographs for reproduction permitted by Dreamstime.com

China National Publications Import & Export (Group) Corporation is an authorized distributor of
Oxford Elementary Chinese.

Please contact content@cnpiec.com.cn or 86-10-65856782

ISBN: 978-0-19-082145-6

10 9 8 7 6 5 4 3

Teacher's Edition
ISBN: 978-0-19-082157-9

10 9 8 7 6 5 4 3 2